T0381455

What people are saying:

"Brandon Baumgarten is a man of God with integrity that he walks out before people. When I first met him, I recognized quickly that Brandon was a person who takes his walk with the Lord seriously. We spent a season together, during which I had an opportunity to speak the word into his life. Mature beyond his years, Brandon clearly spends time at the feet of Jesus! I highly recommend *Habitat for Holiness*. It is a well-written book that will truly help anyone who will read it!"

—Dan Yankunas, Senior Pastor, Solid Rock Church

"I love this book! One of the best I have read in my fifty-two years of ministry. I proudly call Brandon Baumgarten one of my spiritual grandsons, and I highly recommend you take the time to read *Habitat for Holiness*. This reading will give you new insights concerning holy living and purity of heart, written by a millennial who is speaking to his generation and beyond what true life is all about."

—Dale Gentry, Founder of the Breakout Prayer Radio Network and the Let's Pray America Initiative

"This book is so good! I love the concept of cultivating a life and habitat that is hungry for God's word and willing/desiring to hear His voice. Brandon does a great job of laying out how to create and encourage that habitat to become more willing and inviting to hearing God's word and promises. I really love it! God's word is revealed brightly. Thank you, Brandon, for listening to his calling to feed a hungry society."

—Shannon Norris, Zig Ziglar Legacy Certified Presenter & Habitudes Certified Facilitator

"Annual checkups are very important for health, business, machinery, and everything else we deem important enough to ensure proper functioning. Brandon's newest book, *Habitat for Holiness*, is a well-rounded checkup for your soul. Through his unique eye to recognize Jesus in everyday life, Brandon unites God's word and relatable life experiences to encourage each of us to open our hearts and allow Jesus to create a *Habitat for Holiness* in us."

—Lee Witt, Senior Pastor, Hazel Dell Baptist Church

"Brandon does an outstanding job of articulating how to cultivate the habit of holiness and defining what habits hinder a person from being holy. This book is not only well laid out but gives a person a great start in a biblical understanding of being one mind with Christ in body, soul, and spirit."

—Mike Jestes, Chairman, Oklahoma National Day of Prayer

The Habitat for Holiness
Cultivating a Christ-Like Lifestyle

BRANDON BAUMGARTEN

WESTBOW
PRESS®
A DIVISION OF THOMAS NELSON
& ZONDERVAN

WestBow Press books may be ordered through booksellers or by contacting:

WestBow Press
A Division of Thomas Nelson & Zondervan
1663 Liberty Drive
Bloomington, IN 47403
www.westbowpress.com
1 (866) 928-1240

ISBN: 978-1-9736-7267-8 (sc)
ISBN: 978-1-9736-7269-2 (hc)
ISBN: 978-1-9736-7268-5 (e)

Library of Congress Control Number: 2019913048

Print information available on the last page.

WestBow Press rev. date: 8/29/2019

Contents

To the late Reverend William Ryan, or "Uncle Bill," as I grew to know him as, who passed away just a few months before this book was published. If there is anyone who cultivated a habitat for holiness, it was him. Uncle Bill, I am grateful for your heart and for sharing so many spiritual lessons over the course of my life. It was an honor to show this book to you before you made it to glory. Heaven gained a warrior, and because of your obedience to God, generations of our family and friends have been positively impacted for eternity. Thank you, Uncle Bill, for listening, heeding, and being attentive to the still, small voice.

Pictured above, from left to right: Donna Ryan,
Uncle Bill Ryan, Brandon, and April.

FOREWORD

by Tom Ziglar

Over the last several years, I have gotten to know Brandon Baumgarten as one of our Ziglar Legacy Certified speakers. One of the reasons I admire and respect Brandon is that he is a man of action who leads with a servant's heart. I believe you are really going to enjoy getting to know Brandon through his book, *Habitat for Holiness*.

The title of the book really got my attention. The word *habitat* contains the word *habit*, and I have made it a habit for the last three years to learn everything I could about the power of good habits! Good habits will certainly create a good habitat, and what habitat can be better than one that draws you closer to God? Yes, if you want more out of life and to discover how you can draw closer to God, this book is for you.

Think of it this way:

> *Fig trees bear figs.*
> *Apple trees bear apples.*
> *A tree's fruitfulness depends on its root-fullness.*

Just like the quality of fruit from a tree, the fruit from our lives depends on how we nourish our roots. A healthy tree with well-nourished roots bears beautiful fruit and provides a great habitat for many of God's creatures. Our lives are the same way. When we create the habits in our lives that nourish the roots of our character, not only does our life bear beautiful fruit, but we create a habitat or God that benefits ourselves and His children.

We know for certain that life is tough and that storms will come. We know that there will be seasons of floods, high winds, and drought. Yet, when we take time to nourish our roots so that they grow deep and strong, the trials we face only make the fruit sweeter and more fulfilling. As you read this book, take time to reflect and to implement the habits that Brandon talks about. Creating a *Habitat for Holiness* in your own life is a choice. Choose to win!

Sincerely,
Tom Ziglar, CEO of Ziglar, Inc. and proud son of Zig Ziglar

PREFACE

From the Heart of an Imperfect Christian

Never once in my life have I been a perfect Christian or a perfect man. I have sinned so many times and done countless things contrary to what God expects of His followers. I write this book knowing I had the past of a great sinner but fully believing I have been forgiven by a mighty Savior. After over twenty years of walking with Jesus, I'm convinced there is nothing that can compare to truly knowing Him.

As a pastor's kid, my experience might be different from that of most Christians. I heard the gospel all through my childhood, and often the sermon I heard all throughout the week was likely to be the sermon I would end up hearing the upcoming Sunday morning at church. I gave my life to Christ when I was four years old, and I've never regretted that decision. My parents, through their love and desire to see my siblings and me honor God, were among the greatest influences in my life and spiritual walk. There have been many stories told of so-called preacher kids rebelling. By God's grace, my siblings and I have chosen not to reject the message of the gospel but instead to run with it.

As a child, I would often ask my parents about the people we met or interacted with, curious to know whether they had a relationship with Jesus. Whether it was someone we saw on the street, a construction worker, a Wal-Mart employee, etc., they would always reply with, "Well, we hope so." It was the most popular question I would ask, because I knew it was the most important decision anyone could make. By the time you complete this book, I am hoping you have an answer to that question, and my wish is that you will be able to answer it with more than just "Well, I hope so." Because there is no better time to know who Jesus is than right now.

This book had been burning on my heart for years, long before I put it to paper. It had been building every time I dug into God's word, until I could no longer contain it. *The Habitat for Holiness* was born out of prayer, and I pray that the pages not only step on your toes from time to time but also draw you to a closer and more intimate relationship with God. While writing this book, I experienced such a spiritual breakthrough in my own life. I realized that I was writing this book not only for others but also for my own growth as a believer. Our Lord and Savior gave everything He possibly could to give us the gift of salvation. After all He has done for us, I feel compelled to give everything I have to follow Christ and obey His will.

Throughout this book, we will cover ten specific chapters of spiritual growth integral to cultivating a holy lifestyle. I believe the habits outlined in this book are critical to our walk and that every person (myself included) can deepen his or her spiritual habitat for Christ. Jesus wants more than our emotion; He desires our devotion. This devotion to Christ happens when we make our habitat a habit, the integration of faith lived out in a consistent daily pursuit of knowing Him more. Every human has basic essential needs, such as water, food, and air, among other things. We make certain we have these essentials because they are necessary to our survival. However, I believe there is no greater essential need to mankind than Jesus Christ. He is the Premier Essential to each of our lives, because without Him, we are bound for a life of destruction, and eventually the ultimate destination of eternal hell. Therefore, the need to cultivate a holy habitat for Him cannot be overstated. Jesus is everything, and as long as we breathe oxygen, we have a spiritual habitat He wants to use. Will we allow Him to do so?

From the heart of this author, I have one main goal for you as the reader: *to understand that we were made to glorify Christ in every area of our lives—to know we must make room for Him by cultivating a lifestyle which honors His name.* We are called to be ambassadors of Christ; what we do, what we say, and how we live are all a reflection upon Him. I plead with you as the apostle Paul pleaded with the Church in Romans 12:1 (NLT): "And so, dear brothers and sisters, I plead with you to give your bodies to God because of all he has done for you. Let them be a living and holy sacrifice—the kind he will find acceptable. This is truly the way to worship him."

May this book help you understand your value in Christ, know your role in Christ, and strengthen your personal walk with Christ so that you may live your life as a living and holy sacrifice—as a holy habitat—for Christ to dwell in you!

In Christ,
Brandon, an imperfect Christian

"The cross shows us the seriousness of our sin, but it also shows us the immeasurable love of God."

—Reverend Billy Graham

CHAPTER 1

Sin—The Pollution of our Habitat

But God demonstrates His own love for us in this;
in that while we were still sinners, Christ died
for us.

—Romans 5:8 (NIV)

"Devastating."

That was the word many newspapers and media outlets used to describe the situation on the Gulf Coast. It was 2010, and millions of barrels of oil had spilled into the Gulf of Mexico, killing wildlife, fish, birds, and so many habitats. A once-beautiful, vibrant, charming part of the world had become polluted with oil. Blackness covered the top of the water. The pollution was so great that very little life made it out alive. It took days upon days, weeks upon weeks, and months upon months to clean up the entire mess in the Gulf of Mexico, not to mention the legal ramifications that would follow in the coming years. This devastating situation would forever be known as The BP Oil Spill.

You might be reading this book and wondering what the BP Oil Spill has to do with our walk with God. The fact is we have something in common with the worst oil spill in US history. We are polluted just like the Gulf of Mexico once was—not by oil but by sin. Sin is the transgression we have made against divine law.

It is the deadly poison to our soul and is invasive to our spiritual habitats. The Bible clearly says that the consequence of our sin is eternal death. We must deal with it, because failure to do so leaves us with an inevitable eternity of spiritual destruction. Sin has corroded our hearts and infiltrated our habitats. We were born with sin, and now, more than ever, we need to be cleansed from it. I don't know where you stand with God. Perhaps you were given this book as a gift. Maybe you picked it up at a bookstore. Regardless of how you received this book, I pray that you receive this message: we are polluted by sin, and only Jesus can make us clean.

Some of you may be scratching your head and thinking, *But how could God ever cleanse me of my sin? I have done so much wrong, committed so many sins, and lived contrary to the way God wants me to live.* Haven't we all? Those thoughts that are going through your mind right now are very common, but they are totally false. We serve the God of love, and even though He sees the depths of our sin—the total impact of what we have done wrong—He still loves us and is willing to forgive. In Romans 5:8 (NIV), it says, "But God demonstrates His own love for us in this; in that while we were still sinners, Christ died for us."

You see, God knew we would be polluted by sin. Our habitats would be unclean, but God sent us a hope that is brighter than tomorrow. This hope is Jesus Christ, and whether you are a new Christian, you are a veteran Christian, or you've never even heard of Jesus before this book, *we all* need more of Jesus in our lives. Sin pollutes our habitat because it is a swamp to our life, corroding our hearts, feasting upon what is good, and fostering all that is contrary to a holy life. *Repent of your sin and let God eradicate your polluted habitat.* If we desire to live a holy life that is pleasing to God, we must deal with the dirtiness of habitat. Even many of our churches today are filled with people who have never once dealt with their sin. It's easy to sit in a pew and look the part, but even though many folks look clean on the outside, they are bound for an eternity in hell because they have failed to deal with the pollution of sin on the inside. We must allow God to clean up our hearts, for only He can truly cleanse us.

You might say, "Brandon, how could God love me enough to help me in spite of all the things I've done against Him?" The answer to that question is so profound, I don't think I could do it full justice here. God knows your value, but do you? God values you so much He was willing to go the extra mile so we could receive salvation from our sin. God values you because of how much He loves you.

Although I cannot fully describe how much God loves you, I can give you just a small glimpse of it. The most popular scripture in the Bible is John 3:16 (KJV): "For God so loved the world that He gave His only son, that whosoever would believe in Him should not perish, but have everlasting life." This world hates God; in fact, our history shows we want nothing to do with Him. However, God looked at this world, and He loved us. Even in the midst of our sinful ways, He "so loved us." If you were look up the word "so" in Webster's dictionary, you would find this definition: "to such a great extent." Are you getting a hold of this yet?

God loved us to such a great extent that He gave His only son to die for us. Because the pollution of our sin was so great, it required the ultimate sacrifice for us to be clean. He gave us His only son. He didn't sell his son. He didn't auction Him off. Instead, God literally *gave* his only son. He gave us Jesus so that whosoever believes in Him would not perish but have everlasting life. In this wording, the term *whosoever* applies to anyone, regardless of social status, bank account balance, athletic ability, heritage, background, etc. Whosoever believes in Him shall not perish but have everlasting life.

You see, the love of God is so distinct, so uncommon, and so incredible. He looks at this world, inhabited by sinners like you and me, and says, "I love you. Spend eternity with Me." We are polluted, and there is nothing human hands can do about it. The pollution of sin corrodes our hearts, but the grace of God cleans us and makes us new. Once again, I say to you, *"Repent of your sins and let God eradicate your polluted habitat."* Give your heart to God, and allow Him to do the work that only He can do. God didn't have to make the way to cleanse us from our filth, but I'm so thankful He did. We were all polluted, but God stuck His hands in the mud of our mess, pulled us out, and made us new again. With sin, we are dirty like the polluted Gulf of Mexico once was, but with God, we are cleaner and shinier than the brightest pearls in the ocean.

Chapter 1: Habitat Hindsight

Friend, before you read any further in this book, I implore you to repent of your sins, get on your knees, and allow God to eradicate your heart's pollution. He is always listening and desires a relationship with you. After you pray, write down below what you felt God was saying to you during this chapter. What can you apply to your walk with God? There is no right or wrong answer. Just tune into Jesus.

_____

_____

_____

_____

_____

_____

_____

_____

_____

_____

_____

_____

_____

_____

_____

_____

_____

_____

_____

The world out there is not waiting for a new definition of Christianity; it's waiting for a new demonstration of Christianity.

—Reverend Leonard Ravenhill

CHAPTER 2

What Is My Habitat?

The Lord is my strength and song, and he is become
my salvation: he is my God, and I will prepare him
an habitation; my father's God, and I will exalt him.

—Exodus 15:2 (KJV)

I was stumped!

It was 3:30 on an early Sunday morning, and I hadn't slept a wink. My dad had been praying throughout the week and believed I was supposed to deliver the upcoming Sunday-morning message. I had been scrambling all weekend to come up with anything to speak on (those who know me know I rarely lack anything to say). I had preached at the church many times, and for as long as I could remember, I never faced as much difficulty preparing for a message. But this time was different!

Saturday night, I was bound and determined to come up with a topic, but I never felt the leading of the Holy Spirit. I stayed up the whole night, searching, praying, studying, and looking at old notes, and still, nothing came. Finally, the mental fatigue was all I could stand. I fell on my knees and prayed as I had never prayed before. I cried out to God. I vividly remember praying, "Lord, give me a word for your people. I am so utterly empty and feel completely useless. Give me a word that will rattle the cages of this world and pierce the heart of your church. My life is not my own. It is yours, and I ask You: give me a word that will impact Your church!"

That prayer led me to this book. Soon after I prayed, God directed me to Exodus 15:2 (KJV): "The Lord is my strength and song, and he is become my salvation: he is my God, *and I will prepare him an habitation*; my father's God, and I will exalt him" (italics added). I pondered this scripture, but I didn't know where to go with it. I learned it was a song of Moses to the Lord, and soon this lyric struck through my heart: "And I will prepare him a habitation." The metaphorical hamster in my head began to start turning on his wheel, and I began to wonder what the word habitation even meant. If you research the biblical definition of the word "habitation," you will find a definition by the *International Standard Bible Encyclopedia*: "Properly a place of sojourn or dwelling."

In other words, *a habitation is a dwelling place*. From the moment I learned that, I could never recall a sermon coming to me so quickly or easily. God began revealing to me that our lives are a spiritual habitat, a dwelling place for Him.

In a similar sense, each of us exists in our own habitat, a spiritual environment that exalts either God or the flesh. In this book, we will refer to our walk with the Lord as the habitat. As believers, we create a culture that either brings glory to God or doesn't. Our spiritual habitat sets the standard for every area of our lives, because it represents the most important thing in our lives: our relationship with Jesus. This habitat can be strong and yield much for the kingdom of God if we are willing to take steps to grow closer in our daily lives with the Lord.

Within our habitat, we have the chance to operate in fruitfulness when we live a life of praise, honor, and glory to God. The Bible says in 1 Peter 1:15–16 (NLT): "But now you must be holy in everything you do, just as God who chose you is holy. For the scriptures say, 'You must be holy because I am holy.'"

We have been urged to live a holy and sacred life, withdrawing from all impurities. It is a pattern of spiritual living we can strive to incorporate with God's help. According to the Ancient Hebrew Research Center, the word "holy" in the Hebrew language is *qodesh*, which translates "to be set apart for a special purpose." Did you know God has a special purpose for your life? He calls us to be holy because He has set us apart. As Christians, we have been called to be a people who are separated from the world—to be in it but not of it. Praise God!

No other condition is as important in our lives as our own spiritual condition, because it affects everything else. The King of kings and Lord of lords longs to live within your habitat. The holy presence of the Lord desires to burn inside you, reside in you, and lead you in the way of His will.

Think about that: God, the Creator of the universe—air, sky, time, space, and everything that lives, breathes, and dies—aspires to dwell within you! You see, this truth alone stirs my heart, because it reveals the loving nature of our Lord. He sees us and calls us as His own. His heart is to be the centerpiece of your life, the focal point of your soul, *the sole inhabitant of your habitat.*

When we recognize our lives as a dwelling place for Christ, we soon recognize a daily need to commune and know Him more. Drawing nearer to Christ results in more intimacy in our relationship. The more we seek Him, the greater our hunger to follow His ways and learn from His heart will be. However, we first must acknowledge who and what is currently living in our habitat today. If you have received Jesus as Savior of your life, you have the presence of the Lord already dwelling in your habitat. If you have not, I once again urge you to get your heart right with God.

The problem many Christians are facing is not an absence of Jesus living in their life; it's the fact they forget Jesus is living in their life. Simply put: we often struggle remembering who is in us because we struggle remembering who we are in Christ. Discovering our identity in Christ allows us to understand His presence dwelling in us. Many Christians have lost sight of their true identity in Christ, and as a result, their habitat suffers. Our habitats are unintentionally neglected when we forget who we are in Jesus, therefore, we never blossom to our fullest potential in the Kingdom of God. We instead lose ourselves, finding our identity in money, pride, politics, power, success, and other earthly things, which will all pass away. However, Christ remains forever! These things are attractive to the flesh, but when our identity is tied to them, our habitat for holiness is crippled. Our walk with God is hindered. An incredible Lord deserves an incredible Church. When we rediscover our identity in Christ, we return to the very reason for our existence: to bring glory to the King of kings.

Although we are called to magnify and bring glory to the Lord, there are many Christians, including myself, who occasionally misrepresent Christ and give our Savior a bad name. When we take our eyes off Jesus and set our gaze upon other things, we bring shame to our Lord instead of bringing glory to Him. We also affect our witness for Christ. I recall one instance where I saw the effects of this in a great magnitude.

Growing up in a small town, I was unaware of all the bountiful goodness of fast-food America. It was not until I reached college that I was introduced to many scrumptious food establishments. However, out of all the fast-food chains I was exposed to, a place called Chick-fil-A stood out. It became my go-to choice for lunch at least once each week, and there, I built many great relationships with the staff and employees. My conversations were always brief, as there was usually a line behind me, so I would order my food, make a connection, and then eat. Now, my goal for this chapter is not to share with you how much of a Chick-fil-A enthusiast I am (that's for another book) but rather to share with you an important teachable moment.

One day, I was going to Chick-fil-A for lunch. As I sat down with my order, I prayed over it and proceeded to eat. Just as I was about to take a bite, one of the Chick-fil-A staff members, who was just getting off work, walked toward me with tears in her eyes and said, "I knew it!"

"Knew what?" I replied.

"I knew you were a Christian because you always pray over your food before you eat."

I confirmed her remarks by telling her I was a follower of Christ not because I prayed before I ate my delicious chicken sandwich but because I asked Jesus into my heart. I asked her how her day had gone. She paused.

"Not good," she said. "Can I be honest with you about something?"

"Yes, ma'am."

"I am not a Christian, but while working the drive-through here, I have met many pastors from lots of different churches. But today, I saw a pastor and accidentally got his order wrong. He received the wrong chicken sandwich. When he realized it, he came back through the drive-through and threw the chicken sandwich back at me angrily."

I'll never forget what she said next.

"If that is how a Christian behaves, then I don't want to be one."

My heart broke for this employee, and I didn't know how to respond. I told her kindly that what she experienced was not the right behavior for a Christian. Then I said, "Ma'am, today you saw a poor picture of Christianity. Nobody is perfect, but if you don't mind, I would love to tell you what being a Christian is truly all about. Do you know Jesus loves you?"

In the next few minutes, the gospel was shared, and her life was changed forever. She gave her heart to Jesus and left Chick-fil-a with a new taste of Christianity—and, most importantly, with a brand-new heart for God.

You might be sitting there thinking, *It's crazy that someone would behave like this. A pastor should have known better than to act that way.* The truth is we are *all guilty* of misrepresenting our Lord, and yes, we all should know better. We might not act that way in a Chick-fil-A drive-through, but we all have done other things that have given Jesus a bad name. We have spread gossip, we have taken the

Lord's name in vain, we have acted poorly at sporting events, we have disrespected people, and we have said things Jesus wouldn't want us to say. Furthermore, we have lied, lusted, stolen, and even remained silent in apathy as a Church. The list goes on and on. These unholy actions bring about an unholy lifestyle, and frankly, they are unpleasing in the eyes of our Holy God. Our habitats are out of order, and now more than ever, we need a change!

I once heard a pastor say there are two things to do with the Bible: "Believe it and behave it!" In that spirit, let us believe the Bible and behave it throughout our walk with God. Throughout this book, we are going to tackle how we can be better at serving our Lord and strive to live a life of holiness that brings glory and honor to Him. The greatest expression of faith we can ever possess is not the presentation of a thousand sermons, the singing of a thousand worship songs, or the attendance of thousands of church services; rather, it is in the example of our individual lives, well lived as a portrait of Christ. Nothing should charm our hearts more than to see the manifestation of God at work. I pray we all come to a point of correction, finding our identity in Christ alone, where we represent Christ the way He deserves, and allow Him to prepare in us a holy habitat where Jesus is truly exalted!

Chapter 2: Habitat Hindsight

Consider these important questions and write your responses below:

1. *"What is my life's identity?"*
2. *"Have I forgotten who I am in Christ?"*
3. *"In what ways, can I live out my identity and better represent the Lord?"*

Ask the Lord to help you digest this message and to be receptive to what He wants to do in your life. Finally, in your own words, write down what the habitat means to you and what you expect God to do for your walk as you read the rest of this book. Let's create a culture that brings glory to God!

_____

_____

_____

_____

_____

_____

_____

_____

_____

_____

_____

_____

_____

_____

Christ really wants a purity of heart, a holiness of the interior life, in His Church.

—Reverend Loran W. Helm

CHAPTER 3

Surrender the Stains: Becoming an Instrument of Purity

> So if anyone purifies himself from anything
> dishonorable, he will be a special instrument, set
> apart, useful to the Master, prepared for every
> good work.
>
> —2 Timothy 2:21 (CSB)

God has an incredible plan for your life!

Perhaps you have heard this statement before, but I do not say it lightly. As you begin to digest the lessons in this book, you will discover the call to live a holy life will become louder and more emphatic. However, we cannot have holiness without purity. Purity isn't just the way we live on the outside. It starts with the heart, on the inside.

God's plan is pure, and He wants a pure and holy people to follow it. Therefore, we must desire a heart of purity, a heart of total surrender that is completely sold out to the will of God. This heart rejects flesh and embraces Christ. Capturing this heart of purity requires us to die to our fleshly desires and yield all we are to Christ. This is difficult for our carnal flesh to hear because it constantly resists. As we yield and allow God to work on the interior of our hearts, we will witness Him working in an even greater measure through the exterior of our lives. He wants to complete His plan for our lives in the fullest extent.

Two Timothy 2:21 (CSB) says, "So if anyone purifies himself from anything dishonorable, he will be a special instrument, set apart, useful to the Master, prepared for every good work."

The call to action of this chapter is to live a life separated from flesh and selfishness. God desires to use us. That's right. The Creator of the entire universe desires to use us as a special part of His work. One thing is certain for me: I do not want to miss out on being useful to the Master. Any moment He can use my life for His glory is a moment I will cherish for eternity, not for pride or boasting sake but to fulfill the incredible plan He has set! However, for us to be of utmost use to the Master, we must strive to possess a heart of purity. How can this happen? Keep reading to find out.

This might surprise you, but my wife and I enjoy shopping. We get to spend time together, and it's a different setting than just simply being at home. Occasionally, we go to thrift stores to see what bargains we can find. During our first few months of marriage, my wife and I did not have a lot of money. My speaking and singing events had not been booking as regularly as usual, and we were doing all we could to pay the bills. Since we were short on finances, we would occasionally go to the local thrift store and see what kind of bargains we could find. On one of our first trips to the store, I was shocked to find the many brand name items, such as Polo, Stafford, and Wrangler, just to name a few. All the clothes there had been previously owned, and the store would resell the donated clothes at their locations.

One day, I decided I needed a new suit jacket for my speaking events. The only one I had in my closet was the same one I'd had since high school. So, hoping to find something cost-effective, we headed down to the thrift store. After much searching, I found a Ralph Lauren navy blue pinstripe suit jacket that fit perfectly. As I tried it on, I looked in the mirror and noticed it had stains all over the back. It was disappointing to see the blemishes, but I still saw potential in it. We paid five dollars for the stained suit jacket and went on our way.

I later took that stained suit jacket to the dry cleaners and asked what could be done about it. They said, "Sir, we can't promise anything, but we will do our best to get the stains out." I did a double take in the window of the cleaners when I returned the next day. I wasn't expecting the suit to look brand new! It gave me a story to tell. You see, when I turned over my stained jacket, I allowed a work to be done—a work that changed every fiber of my suit.

Friend, this illustration might seem trite, but I promise it has a point. Folks all over the world look at their lives and think to themselves, *How could God ever use me with all the imperfections I have? I'm not talented enough. I'm not good enough. I'm too stained for God to use me. My habitat isn't usable.* These statements are all lies from the enemy, as they perpetuate the perfect setup for potential apathy and unbelief. We all have stains, but are we willing to turn them over to God? Are we willing to surrender our stains so we can be made pure and ready to be used? Maybe you have a stain of selfishness, pride, jealousy, entitlement, or something else that's holding you back from the Lord. You have allowed that stain to dictate the status of your habitat, but it is time to give it all to the Father. We must resist any and all fleshly desires and wholeheartedly and absolutely surrender to God's ways. He wants to carry out His plan through you. Will you let Him?

No matter the condition your heart is in – broken, unclean, corrupt, etc. – God sees kingdom potential in you and is faithful to purify your heart. Regardless of your past, the Lord desires to use you as His instrument of purity. Forsake all the things that have stained your life and focus on perfecting your walk with God. We all fail, but the Lord deserves our very all. I will not know every person who will read this chapter, but I believe God is calling you to be His vessel, His special instrument, prepared for every work. Our habitat for holiness can operate only with a heart of purity. Surrender your stains to the One who is known for getting rid of them. Ask God to purify your heart, to help you to deny flesh, and to lead you in carrying out His perfect plan for your life. If He can use a stained suit jacket to change my life for the better, then imagine what He could do with you. Surrender your stains and watch what God does next!

Chapter 3: Habitat Hindsight

Living a holy life requires capturing a heart of purity. Consider this question and write your response below: **What stains in my life need to be surrendered to God?**

Let go of the past and embrace God's future for you. Ask God to purify you and make your heart the place He wants it to be. Pray, "God, help me to be your special instrument of purity so that I might be very useful to You." Perhaps you are wondering what God's plan is for your life. Take some special time to pray and listen to what the Lord is speaking to you. Write down whatever you take away from this below.

_____

_____

_____

_____

_____

_____

_____

_____

_____

_____

_____

_____

_____

_____

_____

_____

A revival is nothing else than a new beginning of obedience to God.

—Charles Finney

CHAPTER 4

Awaken The Habitat

Awake, O sleeper, and arise from the dead, and
Christ will shine on you.

—Ephesians 5:14 (ESV)

"Wake up, sleepy heads! It's time to get ready for church."

As the son of a pastor, I heard this statement echoed every Sunday morning at about 8:00 a.m. As a teenager, I despised these moments, and I tried anything I could to get as much extra sleep as possible, especially on a Sunday. After a couple of failed attempts at waking us, my dad would occasionally move on to another method. Every once in a while, if my siblings and I didn't wake up when he asked, we would soon feel cold water dripping on our faces. Needless to say, we were up within seconds! Looking back, I am thankful for it, because even though it wasn't what we wanted at the time, it certainly was what we needed. We needed an awakening!

Conviction often comes to us in this way. It is never the thing our flesh wants to hear or feel, but it is certainly the imperative sustenance our heart and soul desperately need. This book was written to be true, not to be popular, so many people might not like what I have to say next: I believe, now more than ever, that the Church needs an awakening! An awakening where we open our eyes to all God wants instead of blinding our own eyes to what we want. In my opinion, many habitats have become victims of spiritual hibernation, where we have become asleep to what God wants us to do, because we the Church has not led like it's called to. People are very much alive and capable of doing what the Lord wills, but we have fallen asleep and become disengaged with our spirituality. Christianity has declined in America. In fact, the Pew Research Center showed that from 2007 to 2014, the number of Americans who identify as Christians dropped nearly eight percentage points, from 78.4 to 70.6 percent!

Churches have conditioned Christianity into a glorified hobby, social club, and unfortunately, a place where only the cool people hang out. This is not the church God wants. Instead, God wants a totally heart-driven lifestyle, where desperate, broken, and imperfect people are clinging to Christ every moment of every day. I believe Christianity is not a hall pass to heaven, but a daily homework assignment to reach a world in need. The church was called to be a place where we share and care. Instead, many churches have become a place of wear and tear.

It is abundantly clear that many churches need a wakeup call if we are going to be effective for the kingdom of God. Because if we are not awake, we will never be aware of what God wants us to do. In my view, our society is quickly forgetting the precepts of what it means to live for Christ. We stripped down truth if it offends people. We sugarcoat Christianity instead of allowing the gospel to convict us. The Church has become arrogant in many ways, hindering God from having His way. This arrogance stifles our habitats, because it prevents us from being fully used by God. We live by our own standards instead of God's standards. As a result, millions become ignorant of their spiritual habitat and the victory God has for them. The Church can no longer afford to find itself in a spiritual inertia where we choose to be consistently inactive, stagnant, and resistant to the moving of God. I repeat: **we need an awakening!**

The danger comes in a kind of moral numbness, wherein we

simply ignore the standards and moral ways of other generations because we think they are from the past and do not apply to us. Therefore, we become numb to sin and wrongdoing, because we have accepted them over and over again. When we are asleep in our sin, we find ourselves in a slumber of potential spiritual death, from which only Jesus can wake us. There is a world asleep to the fact God loves them, cares for them, and longs for a relationship with them.

"Lord help us to reach out and become increasingly centered on proclaiming the message of your cross instead of simply occupying a pew on Sundays."

If we desire revival in this nation and in our personal lives, we must ask God to awaken our habitats and hearts to all He desires. It is impossible for us to have revival without repentance. I believe the next great awakening in America can start with just a few people who are ready, willing, and available to be awake to what God wants. Revival can happen, but we must pursue a spiritual renaissance of repentance, righteousness, and rigorous prayer time. We need God to interrupt our plans and open our eyes to His direction. However, just because there are people who are asleep in their walk with Christ today does not mean it never happened in the past. In truth, consider Matthew 26:36–45 (NKJV):

> Then Jesus came with them to a place called Gethsemane, and said to the disciples, "Sit here while I go and pray over there." And He took with Him Peter and the two sons of Zebedee, and He began to be sorrowful and deeply distressed. Then He said to them, "My soul is exceedingly sorrowful, even to death. Stay here and watch with Me."
>
> He went a little farther and fell on His face, and prayed, saying, "O My Father, if it is possible, let this cup pass from Me; nevertheless, not as I will, but as You *will.*" Then He came to the disciples

and found them sleeping, and said to Peter, "What! Could you not watch with Me one hour? 41 Watch and pray, lest you enter into temptation. The spirit indeed *is* willing, but the flesh *is* weak."

Again, a second time, He went away and prayed, saying, "O My Father, if this cup cannot pass away from Me unless I drink it, Your will be done." And He came and found them asleep again, for their eyes were heavy.

So He left them, went away again, and prayed the third time, saying the same words. Then He came to His disciples and said to them, "Are *you* still sleeping and resting? Behold, the hour is at hand, and the Son of Man is being betrayed into the hands of sinners."

After reading this, some might say Jesus's disciples needed an awakening too. They fell asleep in the final moments of Jesus's life, prior to His unjust conviction and crucifixion. My friends, we cannot be asleep when Jesus has called us to be awake. We must desire to live as disciples who are dependent on Jesus, who always trust and obey what the Lord requires us to do. When we become spiritually asleep, we are not fully living. We are instead in a comatose state of deception, carnality, and un-holiness. In addition, we put ourselves in a position to be more susceptible to the attacks of the enemy. My hope is that Jesus will work through anyone reading this and will bring an awakening to their world. Then the awakening would lead to a revolution of this generation and eventually lead others to their freedom in Christ. We can no longer be asleep but instead be instantly ready for God to use us!

Japanese Admiral Isoroku Yamamoto, who planned the attack on Pearl Harbor, reportedly wrote this in his journal after the attack: "I fear all we have done is to awaken a sleeping giant and fill him with a terrible resolve." The admiral was reportedly referring to America as the sleeping giant in the midst of the war. Up to this point, our country had not entered the war. Once the attack hit Pearl Harbor, America was plunged into battle and responded with boots on the ground. The course of the war would completely change with America's rapid involvement and would eventually lead to the Allied victory.

Although some have disputed whether these words were actually written, they do relate to an even larger sleeping giant, the sleeping giant called the Church. Once we wake up and recognize our influence and duty as the body of Christ, there is no telling what the Lord can use us to do! We can no longer allow ourselves to be in spiritual hibernation, where we are susceptible to the attacks of the enemy, dormant in the very moments God is calling us to respond to and ignorant to the leading of the Lord. How can we expect to live a life of holiness when we aren't even awake? Lives are on the line for the kingdom of God, but where is the Church? Now more than ever, we need our spiritual habitats to be awakened and alert to the moving of the Holy Spirit. Otherwise, we will find ourselves sleeping in a proverbial pew, wasting away the short time we have to be God's hands and feet. Ephesians 5:14 (ESV) says, "Awake, O sleeper, and arise from the dead, and Christ will shine on you."

It is my true belief that as our habitats awaken, so will the Church of Jesus Christ. It can start today! With that being said, I hope this prayer becomes your prayer, which shouts and declares to an Almighty God, saying, **"Lord, would You once again awaken this sleeping giant!"**

Chapter 4: Habitat Hindsight

Consider these questions and respond below:

1. *In what ways, am I in need of a spiritual wakeup call?*
2. *How will I commit to be awake to God's leading?*
3. *How will my habitat help others wake up?*

God wants to use you, and we must be aware of His leading. This can only happen if we are awake. Ask the Lord to awaken your habitat and give you a heart to reach people like never before. Pray, "Lord, awaken the sleeping giant within me that I may be the hands and feet of the body of Christ you want me to be. Help me to let go of my pride, selfishness, and anything else causing me to be asleep to your truth." Write down what the Lord is speaking to you right now.

_____

_____

_____

_____

_____

_____

_____

_____

_____

_____

Of all sad words of tongue or pen, the saddest are these,
"It might have been."

—John Greenleaf Whittier

CHAPTER 5

Tidy Up the Temple

Don't you know that you yourselves are God's temple and that God's Spirit dwells in your midst?
—1 Corinthians 3:16 (NIV)

Making the most of a bright and sunny spring break, my wife and I decided to go on a mini vacation to Branson, Missouri. It was greatly anticipated and loads of fun. We saw a music show, ate at Lamberts, and even managed to get a roll or two thrown at us. (Lamberts' fans will get that reference). On our drive home, we decided to make a stop at Missouri's famous Ozarkland Country Store. There are several billboards advertising it all throughout the state, and as soon as I saw one, I took the nearest exit.

Unfortunately, using my internal GPS system (established circa 1992), I found myself on a dirt road with no entrance back onto the highway. I did not know where to go from there except to follow the old dirt road and hope for the best. As I kept driving, looking for a sign of civilization and an opening back on the main road, something caught my eye. We had just passed a curve in the road, when an old, rundown church appeared in the middle of a field.

My curiosity was piqued, and I quickly turned my car into the old parking lot. I parked in front of the church, got out, and looked around. The church was definitely abandoned. Trees and weeds had overrun it. From the outside, it looked dirty, and looking inside through the window, you could see dust and filth. What a shame, we thought to ourselves. That church's capacity to reach people was still there, but its living purpose was no more.

As we looked closer, we noticed an old cemetery just off the way. There we discovered some tombstones dating back to the 1800s. All the while, so many questions were hitting our heads. Why wasn't this church functioning? What made them close the doors? Why was this beautiful place abandoned?

In the stillness of my thoughts, I realized that although this church was built to teach and reach people, its functions no longer existed. It had succumbed to its end with only a handful of tombstones marked in memory. In our walk with God, it's easy to get so busy we forget why we're here. It's easy to give in to the status quo. However, every one of us was built for a purpose, just like that old church. We must not forget the people we are meant to reach. We must live our lives with vibrancy, intentionality, and purpose, because this is the kind of life we were meant to live – a life fully alive for Christ.

I share this experience with you because this old church is like many Christians in our world today. Our lives are dormant, dusty, filthy, and overcrowded with the trees and weeds of this spiritual world. Our life is like a church. In fact, the Bible says we are God's temple. First Corinthians 3:16 says, "Don't you know that you yourselves are God's temple and that God's Spirit dwells in your midst?" If we are God's temple, then why don't we live like it? We need to allow God to tidy up our temples and let Him use us in a greater measure for His glory.

As I prayed over the direction of this chapter, the Lord revealed to me something spiritually significant. Tidying up our temples is imperative to our walk with God. In Matthew 21, we see Jesus enter the city of Jerusalem as people wave palm branches, spreading their garments on a donkey for Him and hailing Him as King. They thought He was arriving as their earthly king, but little did they know He was coming to be the King of their hearts. As Jesus rode in on a donkey, His entrance had already caused others to wonder about who he was. Matthew 21:10 (NLT) says, "The entire city of Jerusalem was in uproar as he entered. 'Who is this?' they asked." The presence of Jesus was so profound the entire town was stirred up and wondered who He was.

Immediately after Jesus went through this jubilant entry into Jerusalem, He entered the Temple and was not—I repeat, *not*—pleased at what He found. In Matthew 21:12–13 (NLT) it's written: "Jesus entered the Temple and began to drive out all the people buying and selling animals for sacrifice. He knocked over the tables of the money changers and the chairs of those selling doves. He said to them, 'The Scriptures declare, "My Temple will be called a house of prayer," but you have turned it into a den of thieves!"'"

Jesus was doing something uncommon. He was cleaning up

the house. He was tidying up the Temple. Now, imagine how big the institution of religion was back in those days. Its influence and impact on society was enormous. One might think what had been going in the Temple had become a normal part of society. However, when Jesus came into the Temple, nothing would be normal any longer, because Jesus changed everything. Why? We see the reason in verse 14: "The blind and the lame came to Him in the Temple, and He healed them." You see, once Jesus cleaned up the temple, He began to do a mighty work of miracles and healing for others, as well as bring glory to God.

Ask yourself this question: If Jesus was looking into my life and was seeing the inside of my temple, would He be pleased? It was not until Jesus started cleaning things up that the Temple began operating in its original purpose. When we allow God to clean up our temple, we can operate in our original purpose. What is currently present in your temple? I know that as I write this chapter, my temple needs to be tidied up. If we fail to take action on this, our temples will resort to looking like the image of the old church I described previously.

If we sincerely desire to cultivate a habitat of holiness, we must withdraw from anything in our lives that is dishonorable, self-serving, or disdainful to our God. It could be an addiction, it could be selfishness, or it could be a sinful habit. Even what we view as the smallest blemish of sin is wrong in the eyes of God. The longer we hold onto these impurities, the harder it is for us to let go of them. Anything within our lives that does not bring glory to God needs to be removed. Because if it fails to bring glory to God, then we must ask ourselves, "What does it bring glory to?"

As I reflect on the rundown old church, I focused on this idea that it stood frozen in time. If we were to examine our temples, would we find an old, rundown, dormant place filled with old relics of a purpose once destined but never operating for that purpose? Or would we find a beautiful temple fully functioning to bring glory to God? No matter the circumstances, He can and will refine your habitat. This life we live is not our own, and the temple we possess was not created for our own purpose but instead to fulfill the divine purpose God has intended for our lives.

Examine your life right now. Ask God to reveal the status of your temple. Are you glorifying God through every part of your life? He is worthy of your maximum effort to do so. Is your temple dusty? God can clean it. Is it filled with anxiety? God can eradicate it. Is it filled with lust? God can remove it. There is nothing too hard for God to take care of. Relinquish the things that are destroying your temple and lay them down at the feet of Jesus. We will only be truly fulfilled in life when we allow God to do what He wants to do in our temple. He alone can restore what we need for us to fulfill the purpose He has destined for us.

If you happen to travel on this old backroad, you will discover this church still standing. As my wife and I left the location and returned to the highway, I thought of the church's potential and purpose, and all at once, I found an old poet's words to be true:

> Of all sad words of tongue or pen, the saddest are
> these, "It might have been."
> —John Greenleaf Whittier

Friend, just like that old church, you too have a potential and purpose in Jesus Christ, and these things are too divinely important to waste. Therefore, we need to let God operate our lives. Let Him clean up our house. Let Him tidy up our temple so He can do an even greater work within us and through us.

Chapter 5: Habitat Hindsight

Consider these questions and respond below:

1. *If Jesus were to walk into my habitat, what would he find?*
2. *Is there anything in my life that might be unpleasing to Jesus?*
3. *What unholy habits are in my life that I need to withdraw from?*

God has the supernatural power to clean up your habitat and tidy up your temple. He wants to do a mighty work within you for His glory. Write down the areas of your life you want God to clean up and improve. There is no issue or mess too big for Him to handle. Be open and honest. Lay it all in His hands.

_____

_____

_____

_____

_____

_____

_____

_____

_____

_____

_____

_____

_____

_____

When we refuse to listen to the still small voice of God, we will look back with regret.
—Pastor William Ryan (Uncle Bill)

CHAPTER 6

Rooted in Christ

Plant your roots in Christ and let Him be the
foundation for your life. Be strong in your faith,
just as you were taught.

—Colossians 2:7 (CEV)

It was a typical afternoon driving through town, until ...
I saw a beat-up pickup truck sitting right in the middle of a busy
intersection with the emergency blinkers on. Clearly, the truck was
having issues. Traffic moved quickly around the sides, driving on
the shoulders. I caught a glimpse of the truck and continued on
my way.

I've got errands to run, I thought to myself. *I'm sure someone else
will help them.*

After scratching things off my to-do list, I went back the way I
came and saw the old truck in the same position dealing with the
same problem. It had been twenty minutes. The driver couldn't
get out while traffic moved on both sides of his vehicle, and he was
stuck in the middle.

I've learned when walking with Jesus, we walk at His speed,
His pace, His timing, and His leading. This was a moment in which
I was just going to have to trust where God was leading. I ignored
the scene once, and this time, the Lord quickened my heart to do

something. I pulled my car over to the nearest parking lot and walked over to the intersection. I maneuvered through traffic and walked to the truck's door. I was nervous and didn't know what to expect. With a deep breath, I knocked on the window. He looked at me and cranked open his window.

Here's the scene: The driver and his family look at me. I see a dad, mom, and four kids seated in the back. Every one of them has a worrisome look on his or her face. The kids are crying, Mom is trying to keep them from panicking, and Dad is stressed out.

"Hey there, you guys need a hand?"

The dad, frantic, says, "My fuel gauge is broken, and we are straight out of gas! Our car stopped right here in the intersection, and we haven't been able to find help. I'm out of money and don't have any cards to use. We were on our way to move in with my father-in-law, but he lives over an hour away from here yet."

I quickly suggested I could help, but we needed to get the car out of the middle of the road. So, together, we pushed the truck just enough to get it out of the way. I told the dad to stay with his family as I went to get them fuel.

When I returned, I could hear the kids celebrating. The mother began to cry tears of joy, and the dad was speechless as I brought the gas can over and began to fuel his truck. After I finished, he thanked me.

I responded, "Sir, I'm happy to help, but the real reason I came over is because the Lord led me here."

He then said, "While we were broken down here, my family and me were praying God would send someone to help us. Before you leave, can you pray with us?"

Consequently, right there on the side of the road, we began to talk about Jesus and then prayed for one another. It was a special time. We finished and then went our separate ways. In hindsight, I'm reminded of an old hymn by the singer Steve Green, called "People Need the Lord." God wants to meet the needs of His children and can use us to meet those needs. You see, when I heard those kids cheering when I brought the gas can down, I noticed I was holding was hope for their moment of need.

God sent us more than a gas can to give this world hope. He sent His only son so we might be saved from our sin. Through this hope, we are set free and rescued from our dooming destiny. This truck was broken down and could not move forward. Many Christians today are broken and need a touch from the Lord to move forward through life. First Peter 3:15 says, "But in your hearts honor Christ the Lord as holy, always being prepared to make a defense to anyone who asks you for a reason for the hope that is in you; yet do it with gentleness and respect" (ESV). As we allow God to lead and prompt our hearts, we can share this life-changing hope with people in all areas of life at the exact moment God desires. Listening to His leading and being open to His plan is the best blueprint to follow as we prepare to share our hope. It just might be that God wants to affect someone through you. I believe every person you meet isn't just another person but a heart God wants to fill and a vessel He wants to use. Therefore, we must yield to the leading of the Lord.

You might be thinking, Brandon, how do we become more aware of God's leading? Over the years, I have felt God lead me in several ways: through the tugging of my heart, in the midst of my prayer time, during a sermon at church, or even simply feeling his direction in a song on the radio. I truly believe God is constantly speaking to us and wanting to direct our steps. The question is, are we taking the time to listen and obey?

Being sensitive and obedient to the leading of the Lord is a green-light signal to the Father, saying, "Lord, I am one hundred percent Yours. Use me in any capacity for whatever, whenever, and to impact whomever You want." The more we allow God to consume our lives, the greater sensitivity we will have to His will and leading. God is looking for an open and willing heart, a heart that says, "Yes!" to His leading and "Amen!" to His plan. To grow more in this and feel God's leading even deeper, we must cultivate a daily discipline of spending time with Jesus. Our spiritual habitat will suffer greatly if the only time we allow God to consume us is at church. Unfortunately, many Christians in America pray and read the Bible only when they walk to their weekly church meetings. No doubt, a deeper walk with God requires a deeper commitment than that of the traditional Sunday and Wednesday services. The sensitivity to the Lord will grow the more we seek him in the quiet place.

Although our time at church is spent among a wonderful community of believers, we must not limit our walk with God to simply a Sunday-morning, Sunday-evening, and Wednesday-evening experience. The spiritual habitats we have need to be rooted in Christ with a fervent desire to heed God's word and apply it to our lives. The greater we are rooted in Christ, the greater our reach for Christ will become. The Bible says, "Plant your roots in Christ and let Him be the foundation of your life. Be strong in your faith, just as you were taught" (Colossians 2:7, CEV).

Let's say a farmer is starting his new crop cycle. He gets in his tractor and begins to plow the ground ever so steadily. With the plowing complete, he starts to plant each seed with the hope of the bountiful harvest each seed will produce. Upon the same day, he waters the seeds and never irrigates the potential crops ever again.

When harvest time comes along, he notices the seeds he once planted never bloomed into the crops they were meant to become. Instead, they scattered, and due to a lack of moisture, they shriveled up. Throughout the crop season, many winds came, and not a single drop of rain fell. All this affected the seed production and resulted in a prolonged drought. "If only I had taken the time to water these seeds, they would have developed the deep roots needed to withstand the winds and lack of moisture," said the frustrated farmer. This potential crop, which was once planted with hope and promise, had now become a disappointing drought.

This illustration reminds us of the importance of being rooted. How can we know what God is leading us to do if we are not seeking

His leading? When someone comes to Christ, it is a magnificent sight. There is an excitement as a seed is planted, but once we commit to begin a relationship with Christ, we must continue the walk by allowing God to deepen our roots. This means praying and seeking God's will, diving into the Bible, and capturing the heart Jesus wants us to have. However, if we fail to irrigate our habitats with the word of God, if we fail to be rooted in Christ, we will find ourselves just like the farmer's crop – going from a seed of promise to living in a spiritual drought.

Allow God to intervene in your life today and help you plant the roots of your habitat in the firm foundation of Christ. I'm still figuring out this walk with God, and I am far from perfect, but there's one thing I know for sure: He can use you anywhere, anytime, and anyplace. If you forget everything you have read in this book, please remember this one thing: *Be sensitive and obedient to the leading of the Lord and stay rooted in Him alone.* The hope we possess in our habitat is not just for us, but we must share it with as many as possible. By developing strong spiritual roots and following God's leading, we can bring the hope of Christ to people all over the world. Because one day, this hope won't just cause people to cheer for a gas can, but instead, they will cheer for the glory of the King of kings and Lord of lords! Stay rooted.

Chapter 6: Habitat Hindsight

Consider these questions and write your responses below:

1. *How deep are my spiritual roots and how will I consistently grow them?*
2. *In what areas of my habitat does spiritual drought exist?*
3. *In what ways will a well-rooted habitat better prepare to minster to others? Reflect and ask God to plant your roots even deeper and irrigate the drought you may be facing. "Lord, deepen our roots so strongly where we are aware of every leading of your spirit." As you pray this over your life, write down what you feel God was saying to you as you read this chapter and how you can be better at staying rooted in Christ.*

_____

_____

_____

_____

_____

_____

_____

_____

_____

_____

_____

_____

_____

_____

Holiness is the joy of our salvation.
—Pastor William Ryan (Uncle Bill)

CHAPTER 7

Carrying the Name

He must increase, but I must decrease.

—John 3:30 (ESV)

When you are in a barber shop getting a haircut early on a Saturday morning, any topic is up for discussion. As I entered the shop one day, there were a few guys chatting over morning coffee. Sports, politics, and TV shows were all up for debate. Soon the conversation went negative. They begin talking about their problems and bad habits while using intense profanity. I did not know what to do except close my eyes and just allow the barber to do his job. Then, all of a sudden, one of the men asked me, "Hey, guy, do you have any bad habits?"

I replied, "The only bad habit I ever had was falling in love with the prettiest girl in Creek County."

They thought it was funny and continued on. Soon, their conversation transitioned to things they hated. Some hated long lines at Wal-Mart. Another one despised overcrowded parking lots. The conversations of complaining and disgust went on and on, until one complaint caught me way off guard, when one of the men said, "Well, the thing I hate the most are those crazy churchgoing Christians. They are nothing but a bunch of hypocrites." It felt like a glass bulb shattered in my heart.

The comment was followed by more profanities. Then the barber cleared his throat and said, "Well, I think Brandon here is a Christian. In fact, I'm pretty sure he goes to church."

Immediately, crickets. A thousand angry thoughts were floating through my mind, and my selfish desire was to lash out, but the Lord gave me self-control at the moment. I took a deep breath and replied, "Yes, I am a Christian, and I do try to go to church, but I am nowhere near perfect."

The man who made a comment replied, "Well, son, I stopped going to church when my father passed away. Over the years, I have decided that church isn't the place I want to be."

I replied with a low voice, "Well, I'll say it again: I'm nowhere near perfect—no church is perfect either—but I will tell you, we do serve a perfect Savior who can help anyone."

He listened to me but never said another word. I invited the man to church and told him if he came with an open heart, God would give him what he was seeking, not as a religion but as a relationship. After my haircut was finished, I left hoping he would see this faith in a new view. Regardless of how the discussion went, I desired that God would get ahold of his heart. I believe every person we meet is not just another person but a heart God wants to fill and a vessel He wants to use. Many people view Christianity in different ways, but I'm praying the world would receive a new revelation of what it means to be Christ-like. When we strive to live a life of holiness, we help the world grasp a deeper picture of what it means to follow after Jesus.

I learned a valuable lesson in this experience: if you claim to be a Christian, you carry the name of Christ. It is a joy and a privilege, but it also comes with a responsibility to reach out and be the body of Christ. My Uncle Bill Ryan, whom I have quoted here and there throughout the book, was someone who courageously carried the name of Jesus as pastor of our church in Oilton, Oklahoma. While I was writing this book, I had the chance to visit with him about this project, and he was so excited for what this book would do. He would often tell me, "Holiness is the joy of salvation." This is true, and we must live it out by uplifting the name of Jesus. People will subconsciously view you in a different light when you say you are a Christian, because we are called to be different than the world. Therefore, we must be ready to proclaim the name of Jesus in any moment. The world hates Christians, but they hated Christ well before that. John 15:18–19 (NKJV) says, "If the world hates you, know that it has hated me before it hated you. If you were of the world, the world would love you as its own; but because you are not of the world, but I chose you out of the world, therefore the world hates you."

Now, one might ask, in a world so filled with hatred, how can we carry the name of Jesus? The truth is none of us can accomplish this on our own. It is through Christ alone that we can do this. Without Christ, I am a weakling, but with Christ, I am His warrior. As believers in Christ, we are called to love this world; a holy people will stand out amongst the crowd of hatred through our acts of love. As corrupt and dark as our world has become, the best way for us to carry the name of Jesus is to exemplify the love of Christ in everything we do. It is not the popular thing to do in the world's eyes, but as we are different from the world, they will soon see the difference in us is Christ. This does not mean we are better than them; instead, we are living life for a greater purpose than our own.

When I think of people who carry the name of Jesus, the first person who comes to mind is the late evangelist Billy Graham. He would preach the gospel to thousands of people all over the world and share the magnificent hope of Jesus. Countless generations have been touched by his obedience to God through his ministry. He was always someone I admired and looked up to. When Billy Graham passed away in early 2018, the whole world took notice. The coverage of his life dominated the news stations for several days, and everyone was talking about the life he lived.

However, all through the media coverage and public discussion that was broadcasted about Billy Graham, one thing emerged above all else: his relationship with Jesus. Folks could not mention Billy Graham without talking about Jesus. Case in point: I recall one news reporter saying on TV in reaction to his passing, "Not only did we lose America's evangelist, but a true servant of Christ as well." His tie to Christ was unquestioned. I believe this is true not only because he carried the name of Jesus but also because he lived a life of holiness throughout the years. His entire life spoke of the love of Jesus. His faith in Christ became his message to the world, and for countless years, I predict people will still be talking about the impact God made through the life and holy habitat of Billy Graham.

Now, I don't bring up Billy Graham to brag about a man but more importantly to brag about Jesus. We have a duty as Christians to lift up the name of Jesus and to deliver His message to the world. Billy Graham is an example of someone who truly desired to be used of God and carried the name of Jesus all through his life. With all the things he did throughout his life, he came to be remembered by his faith in Christ most of all. Praise God!

One day, our time on this earth will expire, and we will move into eternity. After we leave, I wonder what people will remember most about our lives. Will they remember the funny jokes, the good memories, the embarrassing moments, the laughter? I sure hope they remember all of the above. However, my ultimate hope is that we are most remembered for the fiery faith we possessed in Jesus and the way we carried his name while we had breath in our lungs. John the Baptist said it best in John 3:30 (KJV): "He must increase, but I must decrease." Carrying the name of Jesus is an act of humility, because it crucifies our flesh and says, "I want God to be bigger than me in my own life."

Ask yourself, if today was your last day on earth, how would people remember your life? Would you be remembered by carrying your own name or the name of Jesus? Would they know about your spiritual habitat? When we carry the name of Jesus, we pass on the legacy of what Jesus did for us to others. Our lives are a message, and we must ask ourselves, what kind of message is our life conveying to others about Christ? The world will say you are called to be happy, but the Lord tells us we are called to be holy. My life's goal is not to conquer fame but to bring as much fame to the name of Jesus as possible. May the legacy of our lives be consumed entirely with an undeniable walk with Jesus that leaves the world talking about the greatness of our God for years to come. If we want the world to view Christianity in a different way, then we must start by carrying the name of Jesus with honor, humility, and a daily realization that God is bigger than us. Carry on!

Chapter 7: Habitat Hindsight

Consider these questions and write your responses below:

1. *How well do I do at carrying the name of Jesus? How can I improve at it?*
2. *Through what ways have I lived for myself more than Jesus?*
3. *In what areas of my habitat do I need to step back and allow the Lord to take over?*

As followers of Christ, we have a duty to carry the name of Jesus and carry the flame for Jesus all over the world. You might be the only version of Jesus someone may ever see. Pray, "God, help me to carry your name with so much honor so there will be no question about whom I am living for."

_____

_____

_____

_____

_____

_____

_____

_____

_____

_____

_____

_____

_____

_____

_____

_____

We snack on righteousness instead of being filled with it.
—Pastor Lee Witt

CHAPTER 8

Photosynthesis: Focusing on the Father's Business

Blessed are those who hunger and thirst for righteousness, for they will be filled.

—Matthew 5:6 (CSB)

Photosynthesis.

When many people think of this word, they immediately get a flashback to elementary science class. The process by which plants and organisms use sunlight to make food, photosynthesis is essential to growth and life overall. For these living organisms to survive, they must focus on the sun. The same can be said in our spiritual habitats, although we are focusing on the Son instead of the sun. These organisms hunger for the light because they know this is where their sustenance and strength comes from. Our spiritual habitat becomes stronger when we are totally attentive to whom our strength comes from. Focusing on what God wants is critical to the growth of our habitats. What is the hunger of your habitat? Are you focused on your will or on God's will for your life?

In the Sermon on the Mount, Jesus outlined the importance of our spiritual hunger. Matthew 5:6 (CSB) says, "Blessed are those who hunger and thirst for righteousness, for they will be filled." You might be reading this and wondering how you can hunger after what God wants when you aren't able to see what He wants.

Hungering after righteousness requires faith and an appetite to live as God has called us to live. As you seek this hunger, the Lord will sustain and fill you with the essentials you need to enhance and enlarge your spiritual habitat. As we develop this hunger, we begin to understand this principle: we hunger for what we focus on. The more focused we are on God's will, the greater we will hunger and desire after it.

Jesus was constantly focused on God's will. He was mission-minded, always centered on completing the task God called him to do. He hungered after everything God wanted Him to do. He lived his life not to please others but to please only the Father. If we were to look in Luke, we would find even in the early stages of Jesus's life, He had this same mindset. Check out what Luke 2:41–49 (NKJV) says:

> His parents went to Jerusalem every year at the Feast of the Passover. And when He was twelve years old, they went up to Jerusalem according to the custom of the feast. When they had finished the days, as they returned, the Boy Jesus lingered behind in Jerusalem. And Joseph and His mother did not know *it;* but supposing Him to have been in the company, they went a day's journey, and sought Him among *their* relatives and acquaintances. So when they did not find Him, they returned to Jerusalem, seeking Him. Now so it was that after three days they found Him in the temple, sitting in the midst of the teachers, both listening to them and asking them questions. And all who heard Him were astonished at His understanding and answers. So when they saw Him, they were amazed; and His mother said to Him, "Son, why have You done this to us? Look, Your father and I have sought You anxiously."

> And He said to them, "Why did you seek Me?
> Did you not know that I must be about My Father's
> business?"

Think about this: in one of the very first accounts of Jesus, He is already focused on the Father's business. The will of God was greater than His own. This passage of scripture would foreshadow the mindset Jesus would live out even in the coming years of His ministry. He was always focused on God's will, and because of this, He never missed an opportunity to bring glory to the Father.

The world would love to steal your focus and attention from God. However, the more we focus on God, the more we recognize the hunger we have for Him. In today's fast-paced culture, it is so easy to lose our focus on God and turn to our cell phones, TV, playlists, and more. If not properly balanced, these things can become hindrances to our habitat and prevent us from focusing on what really matters: the Father's business. As I write this, I am speaking not only to you but to myself. This is a message I need to hear. We are all guilty of focusing on things other than God's will. If we are not cautious, our focus on God will dwindle, our hunger for God will become numb, and sadly, the Lord will not be able to have His way in our habitats. I am reminded of a story about a profound painter who God used to paint a very telling picture.

There was a painter who was very gifted at the work he did. God would reveal to Him beautiful images in his mind, and he would begin to paint what the Lord showed him. People would always marvel at how magnificent his paintings turned out. You could sense the anointing of the Lord in every display he painted. One day, the Lord revealed to him a picture which burdened his heart greatly.

As he began to paint it, He took more time than usual to make sure every stroke of his brush did the image justice. Once completed, he stepped back and viewed the entire painting in its finished form. In this painting, you could see a beautiful sanctuary with hundreds of pews and lots of people there chatting amongst themselves. Everything in the church seemed to be perfect, until you noticed, off to the side, a small white figure in the very back corner of the sanctuary with its arms crossed. The demeanor of the figure is sad, with tears running down his face.

The white figure was Jesus. He felt restricted in the back of the room due to the people choosing to focus on themselves instead of focusing on God. Simply put: as big and beautiful as this church was, Jesus could not have His way in it. The people were not hungry for God; nor were they focused on the Father's business; instead, they were consumed with their fleshly desires. In everything we do, Jesus *must* become the focal point of our lives. We give Jesus second place in our lives when our world revolves around anything other than Him.

Let me ask you a few questions: How focused are you on Jesus? Are you focused on what God wants for your life? What are you hungry for? Maybe you have lost sight of your relationship with God and need to be refocused. Perhaps you have been focusing on things other than the Lord. Permit the Savior to turn your eyes to Him. Just call out the name of Jesus, and He will do exactly what you need.

I think back to the process of photosynthesis and how it takes the sun to help those plants and living organisms make food. It is a remarkable process! However, do you know what is even more remarkable? It is the fact we can turn to the Son at any time, and He can fill us with all that we stand in need of. Church, it's time for us to hunger for the Lord. It's time for us to desire His will over our own. Most of all, it is time for us to be like Jesus and focus solely on the Father's business, as we have been called to do.

Chapter 8: Habitat Hindsight

Consider this question and write your response below:

1. **Is there anything I desire more than God? If so, what is it?**

Write down those desires one at a time, but leave the first line blank. Empty your heart. Then pray, "Lord, give me a hunger, a true desire for You and Your ways. Help me to focus more on You and what You want me to do. Give me an appetite that desires You above anything else in this world." After you have done this, write "Jesus" on the very top of your desires list.

_____

_____

_____

_____

_____

_____

_____

_____

_____

_____

_____

_____

_____

_____

No man is greater than his prayer life. The pastor who is not praying is playing; the people who are not praying are straying.

—Reverend Leonard Ravenhill

CHAPTER 9

Plowing the Ground

Lord, teach us to pray, just as John taught his disciples.

—Luke 11:1(NLT)

When writing this book, I had several goals for what I hoped people would get from it. I hope that you are taking away deep spiritual lessons that will form healthy habits for your habitat over time. In this chapter, we are focusing on a subject area I believe is greatly talked about but not popularly incorporated into our lives. That subject is prayer.

When a farmer prepares to plant his crops, he usually has to start out with some very challenging work: plowing the ground. He breaks up the soil so the seed will be able to yield more. I have always viewed prayer as plowing the ground. Through prayer, we are breaking through the atmosphere of flesh and seeking spiritual intimacy with the Father. We are praying to continue to build the relationship with the Lord, ask for His help, and listen to His voice.

It was a bright sunny Oklahoma afternoon. I was grabbing a bite to eat when I heard a mother and her daughter praying over their food. It wasn't your normal prayer. As they prayed, I overheard them mention specific areas they wanted God to touch—in their lives and the lives of others. By the time the prayer was over, my heart was stirred, and I desired to pray the way they did. As I was leaving the restaurant, I walked over to their table and greeted them by asking how their meal was. They both said it was great! I then proceeded to tell them, "I couldn't help but overhear the prayer you prayed before you ate. Didn't mean to eavesdrop, but it encouraged me so much! Thank you for being an example of how we all should be."

The daughter looked at me and said, "My mom," who was sitting right across from her, "has taught me all her life about the importance of praying to God."

I responded, "Well, I know it's something I am trying to improve on personally, and one thing I know is that we all need to do more of is pray more often. Thanks again for doing this."

The mom then responded to me with a smile. "We are Christians. It's what we do."

As I wrapped up the conversation and headed out, I could not get past the mom's response. Prayer is so critical to our walk. Luke 11:1 (NLT) says, "Once Jesus was in a certain place praying. As he finished, one of his disciples came to him and said, 'Lord, teach us to pray, just as John taught his disciples.'"

Think about it. The disciples could have asked Jesus for anything when He was them, but instead, one disciple asked, "Rabbi, teach us how to pray." They wanted to know how to communicate with the Father like Jesus did; therefore, they knew there was power in prayer. I heard a Pastor once say, "A praying church equals a powerful church, but a prayer-less church equals a powerless church." An intentional prayer life creates a spiritual discipline that helps us grow in our walk.

The spiritual landscape of our world needs more prayer than ever before. Although many do not want to admit it, we as Christians do not pray as much as we should. I believe the spiritual landscape of our world could change if all Christians would spend more time on their knees in prayer. The spiritual battles that our habitats face are not fought by the bullets of a gun but by the power of prayer through Jesus Christ. The Bible says in Ephesians 6:12 (KJV), "For we wrestle not against flesh and blood, but against principalities, against powers, against the rulers of the darkness of this world, against spiritual wickedness in high places." The devil wants us to stop praying because prayer draws us closer to the Father. Satan despises anything that is beneficial to our relationship with God because He wants to steal your destiny in Jesus. Sometimes I will sense the devil really working against my life, and I will declare with authority, "Devil, get your hands off my destiny! You have no authority. You have no control over me. Jesus defeated you at Calvary, and you are still defeated today. I rebuke you in the name of Jesus!" I do this because the devil wants to disrupt my habitat, and if I let him do that, I am giving him access to the most precious thing in my life: my walk with Jesus.

Every day, we are at war with the devil, and even though we might not be able to see it with our physical eyes, he is fighting us as hard as he can to poison our habitats and destroy the destiny Jesus has for us. However, although the enemy has an arsenal against you, He *does not* have the authority to attack you. When we pray to God, we are fighting back in the spiritual realm and reminding the devil that he is powerless.

In March 2018, the Oklahoma Teacher Walkout took place. Many educators and legislators were divided on the issue of teacher and school funding. The uncertainty of everything affected so many people, from students to parents. Morale was low in the state during this period. My wife is a teacher, and I saw firsthand the toll it was taking on everyone involved. One night, as I was praying in my quiet time, the Lord impressed upon my heart so immensely to have a prayer gathering at the steps of the Oklahoma State Capitol Building. Nothing political or partisan, just a call for all Oklahomans to come and pray for God's will in our state.

Soon, an event emerged from my quiet time, called "The Oklahoma Hour of Prayer," in which people of all ages were welcomed to pray for one hour for our teachers, legislators, and students. I did not know what God was going to do. All I knew was to obey and see what would happen. We held the event on the steps of the Oklahoma State Capitol Building. We had worship, faith leaders sharing, and then people all over the state through Facebook Live and other streaming videos praying for God to have His divine way throughout these critical times. It was one of the most powerful moments I had seen firsthand involving prayer. People were putting their differences aside and turning to the Lord together. Prayer unites people in both hands and in habitats. As I left the event, I scratched my head and thought, *Could it be that God allows us to go through uncertain times for us to draw closer to Him?* I have no idea what all God did during this event, but I do know there is always a purpose to pray for something and someone. Prayer also opens up your habitat to more leadings of the Holy Spirit. Over the years, I have noticed that the more I pray to God, the more in tune I am with His assignments for me. I remember one time, when I had been praying all week and God led me to my habitat's next assignment.

My wife, April, and I were heading to the movie theater one night to enjoy some time together. We stepped in line to purchase our tickets and saw an elderly man sitting on a bench all by himself. We both waved hello and passed him as we bought our tickets. Being the date night that it was, April went and saved our seats while I went to the concession line to get her snack order. Once again, I saw the man on the bench as I stood in line, and God began to move in my heart to reach out. The feeling of the Lord was undeniable, and I knew exactly what to do. That week I had been praying more than usual and that mush needed prayer time had been preparing my habitat for an encounter. I just did not know what. Nervously, I proceed in line, ordered our movie snacks, and took them to my wife.

"I'll be right back," I said to her as I walked out of the theater.

My heart was on a mission, and the rigorous prayer time had plowed the ground for something spiritually significant to happen. I shook the nerves, took a deep breath, and walked out of the movie theater. Near the gate, I said to the man, "Mind if I have a seat with you?"

"Not at all," he replied.

I started with the mission right off the bat. "Sir, I couldn't help but notice you were sitting on this bench alone. No one should be alone at the movies. Would you like to join my wife and me for the movie? We'll be glad to buy your ticket," I said.

The man chuckled at the offer and said, "That might be the nicest thing anyone has ever offered to do for me. But I'm not much of a movie person. I appreciate it, though. Now, what's your name, and where are you from?"

I introduced myself and told him I was a speaker who performed different kinds of youth and music ministries. He was glad to meet me. I told him I felt led in my heart to reach out. I proceeded, "Well, sir, if you don't mind me asking, is there anything I can pray for you about?"

He looked at me long and hard. Then he reached into his pocket and pulled out his old flip phone. He handed it to me and said, "Son, look at that screen." His voice began to crack, and his hand began to tremble. Immediately, an old black-and-white photo of his bride popped up. He said, "Isn't she just beautiful? She was my bride, and now she is in heaven with Jesus." Tears began to run down his cheeks as he told me all about their life together. "I could sure you some prayer for peace in my life. She's gone, and I need Jesus to help me."

I sat there quietly and put my hand on his back. "Sir, I'm willing to pray with you right now."

He and I both closed our eyes on that bench. Even as the moviegoers kept passing by, we prayed right there for the Prince of Peace to comfort him.

The man said, "Thank you, son. Thank you for blessing me tonight."

I said, "Well, sir, the offer still stands. If you would like to come watch that movie with us, you are more than welcome."

He surprised me, saying, "Well, son, I appreciate it more than you know, but the truth is I am the owner of this movie theater, and I never watch the movies."

I shook his hand, and back into the theater I went. Although I went to the movies for entertainment, I realize now that my wife and I were there for more just than a movie. We were there for a mission God had been preparing me for through the prayers I was having with him.

Did you know God has daily assignments for you? Through constant prayer, we can allow Jesus to ready our hearts for every person He wants to affect through our habitats. The closer I draw to God in prayer, the more I recognize His voice and feel His leadings to reach out to others, just as it happened that one night at the movies.

No matter how long were recently we have been saved, we *all* need to improve our prayer lives and impart this habit to the next line of believers. Showing them the need for a spiritual prayer life is so important because it imparts the priority of prayer to the next generation. We need to plow the ground spiritually. Every relationship requires communication, and prayer is our communication channel to God. Whether it is shouted in a microphone or said in the silence, God hears every prayer we pray. Often, our prayer lives say, "Lord, give me. Give me. Give me," when we should be shouting, "Lord, use me. Use me. Use me."

Adopting a daily prayer life is not easy. Our flesh despises the idea of spending more time with God. However, the goal of consistent prayer time is not to cross off a wish list or to summon God simply to grant our every request. The goal is to draw closer to God and to continue to grow a relationship with Him. There is something spiritually significant about getting alone and communing with God. Make it your mission to set aside special time each day to pray. It will help you stay focused on your walk and will help you become more acquainted with the heart of God. As we pray to Him, we learn more about Him, and as we learn more about Him, we will desire to live even more for Him.

When I first started praying on my own time, I would simply ask God to intervene in occasional circumstances. I would request Him to help me here and there. However, the more I pursue God in prayer, the more I realize the need for Him in every waking moment of my life. In truth, the best prayer times I have ever had were not the ones when I came with a request but when I simply came quietly, empty, and willing to listen to what Jesus wanted me to hear.

Prayer has to be a top priority in our habitats. It is easy for us to pray to God when we need something or have a certain request. Many people will pray only when they are in dire need of something from God. Although we can ask anything in His name, I believe that if we are to plow the ground deeper in our habitats, we must pray beyond prayer requests. God isn't looking for a placing in your life. He is looking to be *the* priority in your life.

We must stop treating Jesus as our genie and starting treating Him as our one true God. In our relationship with Christ, the true joy is not just in being the recipients of His goodness, grace, and mercy but also in the transformational process of becoming the holy people God wants us to be. When we pray and set aside time for God, we are allowing Him to speak to us and cultivate within our habitats an identity of holiness. It is impossible for us to live a holy life without spending time with the Holy God. Ask yourself this question: "Who am I becoming as I pursue God in prayer?"

Habitual prayer time says: "I'm willing to spend special time with the Lord daily. I'm plowing the spiritual ground because I believe God is wanting to use me in a specific time, place, and season." The more we pray and communicate with God, the more personal our relationship with Him will be. What is Jesus saying to you? Are you willing to set aside special time to listen to Him? The clock is ticking, and the need for us to become active prayer warriors is larger than we realize.

When we adopt a consistent prayer life and people ask why we pray so much, we can respond just like the mom did at the restaurant: "We are Christians. It's what we do!" And I believe God will use our habitats to impact even more people. Perhaps they will be at a grocery store, a concert, or even at a movie theater. No matter where God leads us, prayer draws us closer to Him and to the spiritual assignment He has for us. So let us pray with uncommon boldness and unrestricted time slots. Let's plow the ground. Let's rebuke the devil, let's draw closer to the Father, and let's spend time in prayer, becoming the holy people our Holy God desires.

Chapter 9: Habitat Hindsight

Consider these questions and write your responses below:

1. *What does my prayer life look like? When was the last time I plowed the ground in my habitat?*
2. *How often am I seeking God's voice?*
3. *In what ways, can I improve my daily prayer life?*

Pray for God to help you create a daily habit of praying continuously. Say, "Help me, Lord, to commune with you in prayer." Find a private room in your home, grab some sticky notes, and write out the areas where you want God to intervene. Post them over the walls of the room. Pray consistently over them and watch what God will do! Take each note down as God intervenes.

_____

_____

_____

_____

_____

_____

_____

_____

_____

_____

_____

_____

True prayer is neither a mere mental exercise nor a vocal performance. It is far deeper than that – it is a spiritual transaction with the Creator of Heaven and Earth.

—Charles Spurgeon

CHAPTER 10

The Heart of the Habitat

> And he said to them, "Go into all the world and
> proclaim the gospel to the whole creation."
> —Mark 16:15 (ESV)

"Speak to me, O God. I want to hear your voice. Give me some direction as to what to do next. I can't live this life on my own. Speak to me where I can know it is You!"

This was a prayer I vividly remember praying one night in the spring of 2016 before heading to bed. I was getting ready to finish my last year at Oklahoma State University and complete a bachelor's degree, a long-awaited goal. I did not know what I would be doing next in terms of my career. Lots of doors had been opening, but I was not certain which one to choose, so I turned to the Lord for guidance. Little did I know, He was about to rock my world. This experience I am about to share with you is one not very many people know about, including many of my friends. However, after praying, I felt led to share this story to reveal the heart of this book.

The next day, I got in my car and start driving to school, as I did every day. As I began my commute, I listen to my daily dose of Dave Ramsey financial insight on the radio and started sipping on my bottle of water.

Just another day, and just another morning routine, I thought.

Suddenly, a bright light shined onto my face. My body began to tremble uncontrollably. I found myself losing control of the vehicle, and not a single sound could be heard from my radio, car, or anything else. Everything had gone quiet. I soon found myself leaning in my driver's seat with an overwhelming sense of peace. It was as if everything had stopped. No doubt I was experiencing an epiphany like never before.

I did not know what was happening until I heard a sweet and strong voice. It was unique, but I knew it at the start of the voice it belonged to the Lord. As he spoke, I could feel His tone amplified in my chest. It felt like the type of amplification you would normally feel at a big concert, where your body resonates the sound. The voice was calm, soothing, and tranquil. As I listened to the voice, I heard two words repeated to me three times loud and clear: "Feed them. Feed them. Feed them."

All I could do was say, "Yes, Lord. Yes, Lord. Yes, Lord."

I was overwhelmed with a feeling of awe and euphoria. The presence of the Lord had overtaken me, and I sensed the loving direction of the Shepherd. Then, suddenly, the sound of the radio came back on, and my eyes were filled with tears. I found myself still driving and back in control of the wheel. After I finally caught my breath and composure, I began to worship the Lord and thanking Him for answering my prayer.

Even though this experience was mind-blowing, I had a renewed faith in Jesus, and I clung to my belief in Him stronger than ever. Some may think it sounds crazy, but I wholeheartedly believe this was Jesus speaking to me. He answered the prayer I had prayed the night before and revealed Himself to me. I received this word from God, and then He began preparing my heart for sermons, revival meetings, and now this book. He stirred up my heart, and I pray I never to lose this enthusiasm for His gospel. I pray that the heart and intent of this book stirs your heart and boosts your faith in Jesus Christ. The relationship we have with

Jesus is the most holy and precious thing we have. It is the factor that should matter most to us in life.

But do not let this book be the end of pursuing a holy habitat for God. I pray that this reading spurs you on to step up in your church, live out your faith more boldly, activate your calling, and create a Christ-like lifestyle within your life. This book is not the finishing line but the starting point to what God is calling you to do and the holy life he is calling you to live!

When Jesus was about to ascend into heaven, He left a parting message with His disciples. Mark 16:15 (ESV): "And he said to them, 'Go into all the world and proclaim the gospel to the whole creation.'" People often referred to this scripture as "The Great Commission," and rightfully so, because it gives us a charge to do something with what God has given us. I have found it fascinating that the last thing Jesus gave His disciples before He ascended was a call to action. Our habitats will never be holy if we do nothing to lift up the name of Jesus. We must recognize our purpose in Christ and go do the work He has called us to do.

Every day, the clock is getting closer and closer to the time when Jesus returns. It will be a mighty moment, and I pray our hearts are ready. If, by chance, we do not live long enough to witness this moment, I hope we all will be able to look back at our lives and say, "I did everything I could to bring honor and glory to the name of Jesus. My life has been a habitat of holiness, where Jesus was exemplified and everyone who met me saw Him working in my life." May the seeds of this message take root in your life, and may you realize your role in the kingdom of God. This can all happen by making holy living a continual habit in our lives.

I leave you with one final thought. In Matthew 25, Jesus is talking about the parable of the talents. There were three men tasked with taking care of the master's talents. The first man went and was very prosperous with his talents. The second one did well with his talents, and the third went and hid his money because he feared the master was a hard man. The master was unpleased with the third man because he did nothing with what he was given. However, the master replied to the ones who did take action, "Well done, good and faithful servant."

Friend, one day, we are all going to stand before the Lord, and we will give an account of all we have done here on earth. My ultimate prayer is that when the Master looks at us, those who have strived to live a life of holiness, He will smile and say, "Well done, my good and faithful servant. Here is your reward." May we all come to the place in our lives where the cross becomes our message and our goal becomes glorifying God with everything we have. Jesus is holding out His hand, beckoning you to follow Him and to model His example of living a holy life. The Lord wants to use you in a mighty way, and it all starts within the dwelling place we all possess: the habitat. You have read the book, you have heard the heart, and now you are left with a choice. Will you dare to let your habitat be dormant? Or will you dare to make it holy?

Chapter 10: Habitat Hindsight

Consider these questions and write your responses below:

1. *How will I now commit to living a life of holiness?*
2. *What has happened to my habitat over the course of digesting this book?*
3. *What have I heard God say to me the most while reading The Habitat of Holiness?*

Congratulation on finishing The Habitat for Holiness! *We have covered many different spiritual lessons. Reflect and think back to some things you have taken away from this book.* **FINAL QUESTION**: *How will you apply what you have learned into creating a Christ-like lifestyle in your daily life? Let's continue to make holy living a habit for God!*

_____

_____

_____

_____

_____

_____

_____

_____

_____

_____

_____

_____

_____

> *A holy life will make the deepest impression. Lighthouses blow no horns, they just shine.*
>
> *– Dwight L. Moody*

Social Media Challenge

Has *The Habitat for Holiness* affected your life in any way? Feel free to upload a post to any of your social media sites and share your favorite quote from the book and how this book has helped you. It just might be the testimony someone in your life needs to read in the moment. Use the hashtag **#HabitatHelped** and share your thoughts. Thank you for reading! May God bless you greatly as you pursue him with all of your heart!

-Brandon, an imperfect Christian

Acknowledgments

This book could not have happened without the help of so many people:

April Baumgarten, thank you for helping with youth events, gospel singings, the sound booth, and all my other crazy projects. I owe you so much gratitude and appreciation. Thank you for making me a better man! I love you!

Christian Favalora, thank you for taking the time to edit and proofread, and for offering your creative-writing tips in this project. You da man!

Pastor Bill Baumgarten (Dad), thank you for teaching me the priority of following Jesus and how to live a holy life. I am who I am largely because of you!

Pastor Lee Witt, thank you for mentoring me and for always believing in my endeavors. I'm honored to serve alongside you. If I turn out to be half the man you are, I'll be all right!

Ron Harnden (Grandpa), thank you for your constant interest and belief in all my projects. I can always count on you to be the first to read, listen, and have a pot of coffee ready.

To everyone else, thank you for your prayers, kind wishes, and support!

About the Author

Brandon Baumgarten has been a featured speaker and writer for many outlets across the country. He graduated in 2016 with a bachelor's degree in agricultural leadership from Oklahoma State University, where he started writing for the collegiate newspaper and was named a top-ten student. Since then, he has maintained a busy speaking schedule at churches, conferences, youth groups, and schools, with more than one hundred events each year. His message is always to engage, encourage, and empower others to fulfill their purpose in life. His heart is to see personal revival take place in God's people. He currently serves at his church in Oklahoma as both a youth and music minister. Brandon is also an award-winning soloist in the Southern gospel music and contemporary Christian music genres. He and his wife, April, currently live in Shawnee, Oklahoma, and are expecting their newborn child in November.

For information on scheduling Brandon to come to your church, school, or upcoming event, please visit www. brandonbaumgarten.com.

Works Cited

Hicks, G. (2014, February 24). Awakening the Sleeping Giant: The Birth of the Greatest Generation. Retrieved from https://www. blogs.va.gov/VAntage/11713/awakeningthe-sleeping-giant-the-birth-of-the-greatest-generation/.

Wormald, B., & Wormald, B. (2017, September 07). America's Changing Religious Landscape. Retrieved from http://www.pewforum. org/2015/05/12/americas-changing-religious-landscape/.

Notes

Notes

Notes

Notes

Notes

_____

_____

_____

_____

_____

_____

_____

_____

_____

_____

_____

_____

_____

_____

_____

_____

_____

_____

_____

_____

_____

_____

_____

_____

_____

_____

_____

Notes

Notes

Notes

Notes

Notes

Notes

Notes

Notes

Notes

Notes